This book is dedicated to all the wild animals that have blessed me with beautiful windows into their lives.

Baby Animals
Eating

SUZI ESZTERHAS

Owlkids Books

Baby animals are always hungry! They eat lots of food to get the nutrients they need to grow big and strong. Let's see what these baby animals are feasting on.

These brown bear cubs don't know how to fish or break open clams yet, but they sure like eating and playing with Mom's leftovers.

Koalas are very picky eaters. They eat only leaves from eucalyptus trees for breakfast, lunch, and dinner. And they have to climb up high to get their food. Hang on tight, joey!

A father jackal returns after a morning of hunting. The pups greet him and beg for food by licking his face. Dad will spit up some of the meat he's eaten and share it with the pups.

Dad penguin catches fish, swallows them, and then coughs them up to feed his baby. The chick will eat this way until she can dive into the ocean and catch fish on her own.

Egret parents take turns feeding fish and frogs to their hungry chicks. This greedy chick gobbles all the food from Mom's beak. He doesn't want to save any for his brothers and sisters!

Cheetahs are meat eaters. This mother cheetah is teaching her cubs how to stalk and catch prey, such as gazelles. Later, the family will eat together.

Monkey and chimpanzee babies drink warm milk from their mothers' bodies. Whenever they need a snack, Mom is there. These babies never go hungry!

Fresh green leaves on the treetops are perfect for tall giraffes. This calf plucks juicy leaves with his long tongue. He eats leaves for hours and hours every day.

A mother warthog has many hungry mouths to feed. But Mom has plenty of milk for each and every little piglet. *Gulp, gulp!*

Raccoon kits will eat just about anything they can get their paws on. This lucky baby found a quail egg that he can't wait to crack open.

This mother orangutan mashes up fruit in her mouth and then passes it to her baby. Thanks, Mom!

Sloths eat very slowly. Their bellies also work slowly to digest what they eat. It could take this sloth a whole month to digest a single leaf!

Suzi Eszterhas

I watched this sea otter pup learning how to find clams. Each time he dove into the water, he came up with nothing. Eventually Mom shared her meal with him.

This lion cub has a full tummy! Lions sometimes go days between meals, so they eat as much as they can at once. Every meal is like an eating contest in a lion's world.

Hi, I'm Suzi!

I travel all over the world taking pictures of animals. I also help animal conservationists by telling their stories and helping raise money for their causes. When I'm not snapping photos, I like talking to people about how they can help wild animals. I think it's important for kids to connect with animals and nature. You can do this by looking at photos, reading books, or just going outside and running, climbing, and jumping like these baby animals!

Beavers use their super strong teeth to munch on tree branches. This kit's teeth will never stop growing, even when she's all grown up!

Mommy capybara watches over her young ones while they drink milk, keeping them safe from predators, like jaguars.

This elephant calf is using her trunk to take food right out of her mother's mouth! Elephants also use their trunks to pick up nuts.

This serval kitten lost its mom. While in Africa, I got to help raise him and feed him from a bottle until he was strong enough to be released into the wild. It was amazing.

This panda cub is a little too young to eat anything but her mother's milk, but she likes to chew on bamboo anyway. After her snack, I watched her play panda games with her sister. So cute!

Consultant: Chris Earley, Interpretive Biologist, University of Guelph Arboretum

Owlkids Books acknowledges the financial support of the Canada Council for the Arts, the Ontario Arts Council, the Government of Canada through the Canada Book Fund (CBF) and the Government of Ontario through the Ontario Media Development Corporation's Book Initiative for our publishing activities.

Published in Canada by
Owlkids Books Inc.
10 Lower Spadina Avenue
Toronto, ON M5V 2Z2

Published in the United States by
Owlkids Books Inc.
1700 Fourth Street
Berkeley, CA 94710

Library and Archives Canada Cataloguing in Publication

Eszterhas, Suzi, author, photographer
        Baby animals eating / Suzi Eszterhas.

(Baby animals ; 3)
ISBN 978-1-77147-317-0 (hardcover)

        1. Animals--Food--Pictorial works--Juvenile literature.
2. Animal behavior--Pictorial works--Juvenile literature.
3. Animals--Infancy--Pictorial works--Juvenile literature.
I. Title.

QL756.5.E88 2018   j591.5'3   C2017-907421-0

Library of Congress Control Number: 2017961191

Edited by Jackie Farquhar
Designed by Danielle Arbour and Alisa Baldwin

ONTARIO ARTS COUNCIL
CONSEIL DES ARTS DE L'ONTARIO
an Ontario government agency
un organisme du gouvernement de l'Ontario

Canada Council   Conseil des Arts
for the Arts   du Canada

Canadä

Manufactured in Dongguan, China, in March 2018, by Toppan Leefung Packaging & Printing (Dongguan) Co., Ltd.
Job #BAYDC54

A   B   C   D   E   F

OWL kids   Publisher of Chirp, chickaDEE and OWL
www.owlkidsbooks.com

Owlkids Books is a division of

Bayard
CANADA